Grandmother Remembers Holidays

Grandmother Remembers Holidays

An Album of
Memories and Photos
for My Grandchild

by Judith Levy

Stewart, Tabori & Chang
New York

Published in 2010 by Stewart, Tabori & Chang
An imprint of ABRAMS

Text © 2010 by GENERATIONS, INC.
Illustrations by Christy Taray, © 2010 The Stonesong Press, LLC
Produced by The Stonesong Press, LLC
Designed by Ohioboy Art & Design

Library of Congress Cataloging-in-Publication Data:
Levy, Judith.
Grandmother Remembers Holidays : An album of memories and photos / by
Judith Levy.
p. cm.
Includes bibliographical references and index.
ISBN 978-1-58479-841-5 (alk. paper)
1. Holidays. I. Title.
GT3930.L49 2010
394.26–dc22
2009035051

Editor: Jennifer Levesque
Production Manager: Tina Cameron

The text of this book was composed in ITC New Baskerville and Mahogany Script.

Printed and bound in China
10 9 8 7 6 5 4 3 2 1

Stewart, Tabori & Chang books are available at special discounts when purchased in quantity for premiums and promotions as well as fundraising or educational use. Special editions can also be created to specification. For details, contact specialsales@abramsbooks.com or the address below.

115 West 18th Street
New York, NY 10011
www.abramsbooks.com

Holidays give so much pleasure
in all the things we do
so memorable and precious
because they're shared with you

Dedicated with love to: _____

From: _____

Date: _____

Contents

Our Family

Don't mean to brag,
or even make a fuss.
But I'm just so proud
of a family called "us."

Great Grandmother

Great Grandmother

Great Grandfather

Great Grandmother

Great Grandfather

Great Grandmother

Great Grandfather

Grandfather

Grandmother

Grandfather

Grandmother

Mother

Father

Grandchild

9

I live at _____

_____

_____

You live at _____

_____

_____

Some great things about our family are

_____

_____

_____

_____

_____

_____

Photograph of Family

I shouldn't tell secrets, but your parent always used to

_____

_____

_____

_____

A special memory of your parent is

_____

_____

_____

_____

_____

_____

I was always so proud when your parent

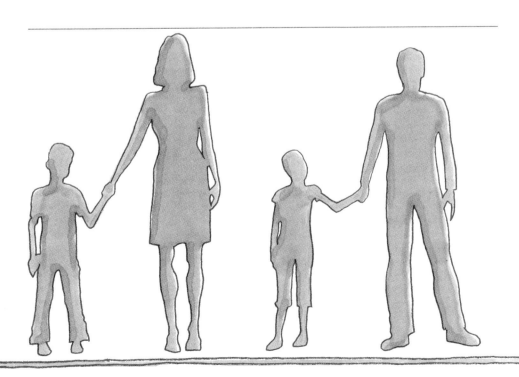

Happy New Year!

The minutes are ticking.
It's getting late, my dear.
For at the stroke of midnight,
the new year will be here.

Date: _____

New Year's Eve is so much fun because _____

_____

_____

We stay up until _____

Our new year's resolutions are _____

_____

_____

_____

Our wishes for the new year are _____

_____

_____

_____

JAN
1

Valentine's Day

Grandchildren are so dear,
especially those of mine.
Precious and so very loved,
the sweetest Valentine.

Date: _____

We celebrate Valentine's Day by _____

_____

_____

I send valentines to _____

_____

Photograph or Valentine

I receive valentines from _____

_____

_____

A special memory of Valentine's Day is _____

_____

_____

_____

Spring Holiday

The weather has turned warmer,
and spring has come our way.
Birds are chirping in the trees
on this sweet holiday.

Date:

This holiday is called

We celebrate this holiday by _____

_____

_____

_____

A special holiday tradition is _____

_____

_____

_____

_____

People who celebrate with us are

We have a delicious holiday dinner that includes

My favorite holiday recipe is

_____

_____

_____

_____

_____

_____

_____

_____

_____

This year what we remember most about this holiday is

Photograph of Family

Fourth of July

It's America's special day,
and there's so much to do.
Come join us and celebrate
at our family barbecue.

Date: _____

We celebrate the fourth of July by _____

_____

_____

The weather is often _____

_____

The people who celebrate with us are _____

_____

_____

_____

Our favorite fourth of July foods are _____

_____

_____

_____

A special memory of the fourth of July is _____

_____

_____

Halloween

All dressed up in costumes,
the cutest I've ever seen,
ready to go trick-or-treating
for a howling halloween.

Date: _____

Last year you dressed up as _____

You picked that costume because _____

_____

You went trick-or-treating with _____

_____

The best treat you got was _____

_____

A special memory of Halloween is

_____

_____

Next Halloween you want to be

_____

_____

Thanksgiving

So many people would join us,
just as fast as they were able,
to be with our wonderful family
around the Thanksgiving table.

Date: _____

We always give thanks for _____

_____

_____

_____

_____

On Thanksgiving we really love to eat

_____

_____

_____

My favorite Thanksgiving recipe is

_____

_____

_____

_____

People who share our Thanksgiving dinner are

The turkey is carved by

A special memory of Thanksgiving is

Winter Holiday

All the children in our house
wish for lots and lots of toys,
special holiday presents
for good little girls and boys.

Date: _____

This holiday is called _____

_____

_____

We get ready for this holiday by _____

_____

_____

_____

We celebrate this holiday by
_____
_____
_____
_____

People who celebrate with us are
_____
_____
_____

We have a delicious holiday dinner that includes

_____

_____

_____

_____

_____

My favorite holiday recipe is

_____

_____

_____

_____

_____

_____

_____

Our gift-exchanging traditions are

_____

_____

_____

_____

_____

It was really fun to see you open

_____

_____

_____

After exchanging gifts, we often

Next year, we hope for

What we'll remember most about this special time is

_____

_____

_____

_____

_____

_____

_____

Photograph of Family

Birthdays

C'mon, we're celebrating!
You're invited to join everyone.
We're having a birthday party,
with cake and a barrel of fun.

Date: _____

We celebrated the birthday of _____

_____

_____

Photograph of Family

Guests were

We celebrated this happy birthday by

The best part of this whole day was

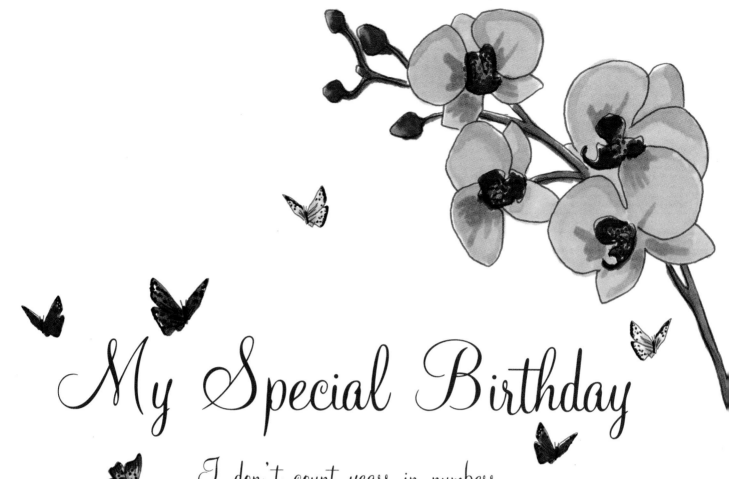

My Special Birthday

I don't count years in numbers,
just the happiness they bring.
And the gift of being your grandmother
has always meant everything.

Date: _____

A birthday I'll remember is _____

_____

It was so special to me because _____

_____

_____

_____

People who celebrated with me were

_____

_____

_____

_____

The best part of the whole day was

_____

_____

_____

_____

Our Wonderful Trip

Off on our magic carpet—
a car, a plane, or a ship.
We discovered a whole new world
on this special family trip.

Date:

We were off to see

We got there by

_____

_____

_____

_____

_____

The people who came on this trip were

_____

_____

_____

_____

What we loved most about this trip was

The best souvenirs we brought back from this trip were

_____

_____

_____

_____

_____

_____

_____

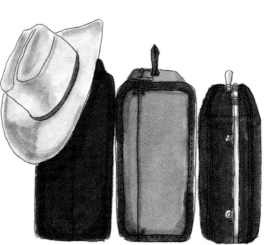

Photographs of Trip

On our next vacation we'd like to go to

_____

_____

_____

_____

_____

A special memory of this trip is

_____

_____

_____

Treasured Family Photographs

*These photos are precious
and will always impart
good times with my family,
so close to my heart.*

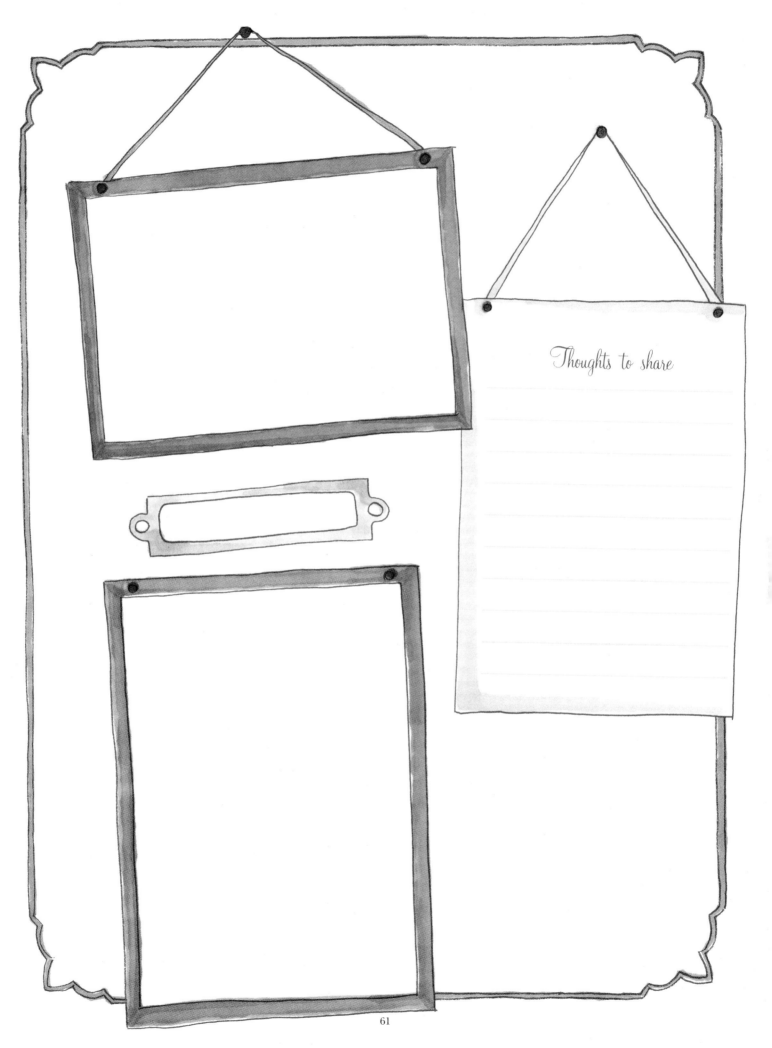

Thoughts to share

Thoughts to share